Pluto

fabula amoris
Teacher's Guide

Miriam Patrick

For use with
Pluto: Fabula Amoris
Rachel Ash
&
Miriam Patrick

Liber Parvus pro Prima Classe Latina

Pomegranate Beginnings Publishing
Lawrenceville, Georgia

Table of Contents

---

[1] These are activities not necessarily found in the book or online teacher's resources. They include a variety of activities that teachers can create for themselves or use as guides.

Introduction

Afterword from *Pluto: fabula amoris*

When Rachel and I decided to write this novella, we were trying to fill a need we felt we had as teachers of Latin students. We knew we wanted to write something that was meaningful to us, but that also could be used by others. We wanted a novella that our students would find compelling and that would fit teachers' many needs.

We settled on the mythology surrounding a pair of deities close to both of our hearts: Pluto and Proserpina, god and goddess of the Underworld. I have long enjoyed the mythology surrounding these two and became even more interested in them when my art history teacher in college described them as the royal couple opposite of Jupiter and Juno. Where Jupiter and Juno were bright and heavenly, Pluto and Proserpina were dark and "Underworldly". Juno was accompanied by peacocks, Proserpina by pomegranates and Cerberus. More intriguing than all this, however, was the pull of the mystery of this love story and just what happened when Proserpina was kidnapped by Pluto.

Our story has a slightly different spin that most we've read. Pluto is not the menacing, daunting man often seen, but rather misunderstood and lonely. Proserpina is not a wholly innocent and unsuspecting girl, but rather one who takes control of her own destiny.

Our version is meant to be a Latin I reader with accompanying pictures, and it contains a complete glossary in the back in alphabetical order. Our hope is that teachers and students alike enjoy this version of the myth of Pluto: a love story.

There are some people we'd like to acknowledge in this work. After writing and rewriting, two people stepped forward to help us edit and review our story. Bob Patrick and Laura Gibbs not only edited our story for errors and typos, but also provided invaluable feedback for our story, its comprehensibility, and how compelling readers would find it. To them we give our unending thanks.

Miriam Patrick
September 6, 2015

How to Use This Guide

This teacher's guide is made to be used in conjunction with the novella *Pluto: fabula amoris*. Additionally, this guide may be used alongside free materials offered online by Pomegranate Beginnings Publishing. The teacher's guide contains suggestions for activities and materials teachers might use while working with the novella.

Throughout this guide you will find a variety of sources you may use with your students as well as a series of short URLs and QR codes. These codes will take you to the materials we can only offer online, like the audio for the chapters and presentations you may wish to use. This book will also contain some materials that are not offered online, such as larger images from the book for you to use. The table of contents for each chapter is color-coded by activity: introduction, listening, reading, and review.

The Usage and Grammar notes provided in this text serve to explain uses of certain words in relation to or instead of others. The resources used for this text include The 50 Most Important Verbs list compiled by the Latin Best Practices yahoo group, Mark A. E. Williams' *Essential Latin Vocabulary*, as well as other frequency lists like Dickinson's Most Common Vocabulary list, and dictionaries like Lewis & Short's *A Latin Dictionary*.

Want to order copies of this guide or *Pluto: fabula amoris?* Check out these and other offerings from Pomegranate Beginnings Publishing by using the QR code or URL: http://pomegranatebeginnings.blogspot.com/p/publications.html

Any questions, concerns, or comments regarding this text or the novella *Pluto: fabula amoris* can be submitted using the QR code or URL: http://pomegranatebeginnings.blogspot.com/p/about-us.html

Usage and Grammar Notes

Page Number	Text	Explanation	References
5	ferociter	Using the definition of "fiercely" to go with amare. While this is not the most common use of *ferociter*, its origin, *ferox*, certainly is used with the idea of love.	*Lewis and Short*'s definition of origin *ferox* and references, particularly, *duas ferocissimas affectiones amoris atque odii coërcere*
6	dicere	*Dicere* is used here to introduce the idea of telling stories. *Narrare* is usually used in this situation. In limiting vocabulary, we wanted to stress mostly words that were high frequency.	In looking in Mark Williams' *Essential Latin Vocabulary*, which lists things by frequency and various other ways, *narrare* has a frequency number of .17 while *dicere* has a frequency number 3.81 with a general meaning of say, tell, or speak.
12	exanimata	Used to reference being unconscious or "out of one's sense"	*Lewis and Short*'s definition and references given in Plautus, Terrence, Cicero, Horace, etc.
15	capere	Used in reference to Pluto's gift. While *accipere* may be better suited here, *capere* was chosen because of its general meaning of "take hold of" and its appearance on the 50 Most Important Verbs list created by Latin teachers on the Latin Best Practices listserv.	*Lewis and Short*'s definition and references given in Plautus, Terrence, Catullus, Vergil, etc.

4

Culture Materials

Outside Resource List

Title	URL	Notes/Suggestions
An antihero of one's own	http://ed.ted.com/lessons/an-anti-hero-of-one-s-own-tim-adams	➜ Opening culture introducing Pluto as an antihero ➜ Opening culture to introduce students to perspective
Nova Roma: Pluto	http://www.novaroma.org/nr/Pluto	➜ Provides detailed notes on Pluto, his imagery, his stories
Class of the Titans	http://goo.gl/YY5vkm	➜ particularly episode 01.04 where Cerberus first appears ➜ particularly epsiode 02.08 where Persephone gets trapped
Seasons Story	https://goo.gl/zvScCF	➜ Written by Miriam Patrick, this story draws from a traditional Iroquois legend and includes the original English. ➜ Use with later chapters to develop cultural understanding of the seasons and various nature mythology.

Questions to Consider

Question/Topic	Rationale	Applicable chapters
Is Pluto an anti-hero?	An anti-hero is someone who does not fit our general idea of a hero, but who fights against the regime/control/power.	All
Why does Pluto talk to Jupiter about his plans?	We see Iuppiter in literature serving as the "end all" power that makes these heavy decisions: Odysseus/Troy, Venus/Iuno/Dido, etc.	Chapters 3, 6, 7, 8
The pomegranate - a gift or a curse?	The pomegranate is a fruit native to Iran that is associated with the gods, wealth, and death. Consider the process to get into a pomegranate: why does Pluto give it as a gift? Is it really to trap Proserpina? Why does Proserpina not want to eat it?	Chapters 4, 5, 7
Cerberus, monster or pet?	Cerberus frightened all who saw him, but he served a particular purpose. Was he truly evil, or was he fulfilling his duties for his master?	Chapters 5, 6
How did Orpheus get his way?	In the book, Proserpina speaks to Pluto and asks him to look kindly upon the mortal. Orpheus uses his music to get past Charon and Cerberus. Did his music have sway over Pluto or did Pluto remember his own story?	Chapter 8
Why does Proserpina choose Pluto?	While a lot is said about Pluto's capture of Proserpina, little is said about how she came to be his queen, other than eating the seeds. What might have gone through her mind? How much power did she hold? How does this compare to the roles of women in Roman society?	All
Pluto and Proserpina - the royal couple	Pluto and Proserpina are often pictured opposite Jupiter and Juno - seated on thrones, covered in regalia, awaiting their subjects. How does this couple compare to the other? Who is, in fact, more royal? Who is the better couple?	All

Solved Mysteries - A Culture Activity

The next few pages detail a culture activity you can do with your students to discover and discuss burial practices in Ancient Rome. This activity works like a running dictation. You can access the directions for this using the QR code below or the url here: https://goo.gl/1IBDUK .

Suggested Rules
- ★ Each person must write all sentences down.
- ★ Group gets one "scaena mirabilis"
- ★ Group must:
  - ○ write down sentences
  - ○ translate sentences
  - ○ identify each item
  - ○ place it correctly on the body
- ★ In the end, discuss funerary tradition

Materials Below
- → Scaena Mirabilis - a cutout of a body that each group should receive. Students will recreate the crime scene with this image.[2]
- → Identify - each group should receive a copy of this to take notes on and answer questions about the scene. This page also has notes for the group.
- → Sentences - These sentences should be posted (half sheets) around the room near the objects they represent:
  - ◆ familia prope corpus posuit - a shattered dish
    - ● represents the last meal the family had at the grave site
  - ◆ erat in manu - a sweet cake or cookie
    - ● to give to Cerberus
  - ◆ erat in ore - a coin
    - ● to give to Charon
  - ◆ erat prope pedes - a pair of shoes
    - ● represents the journey to the Underworld

---

[2] credit for image given to ఇందూ జ్ఞాన వేదిక. Image provided via the creative commons copyright and is located at https://commons.wikimedia.org/wiki/File:Body_Outline.jpg

Scaena Mirabilis[3]

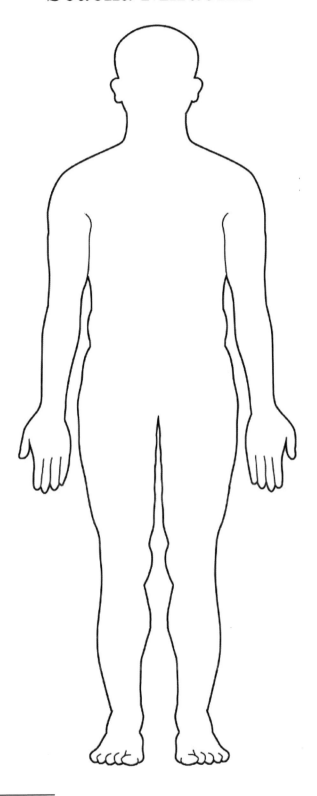

---

[3] credit for image given to ఇందూ జ్ఞాన వేదిక. Image provided via the creative commons copyright and is located at https://commons.wikimedia.org/wiki/File:Body_Outline.jpg

8

Scaena Mirabilis
Identify:

corpus	manus	os	pes	mirabilis
prope	as	calceus	lanx	libum

Explicatio:

1. Send a runner up one at a time to find and deliver sentences.
2. Once you have all the sentences, translate them.
   a. As you find words you do not know, ask your magister/magistra "quid significat" questions.
   b. Record your new word discoveries on both this paper and your own!
3. Then, use the vocabulary to write sentences and draw pictures on your scaena mirabilis.
   e.g. if the piece of evidence was a hat and the sentence was "erat in capite," you'd draw a hat on the head and write, "petasus erat in capite" next to it.
4. When you think you have all these things done correctly, consider the questions below:

Interrogationes

1. What items did you find? What do you know about these items already?

2. Do any of these items/practices seem familiar to you? If so, in what respect?

3. If you could guess what practice you think this whole scaena mirabilis refers to, what would you guess? Why?

familia prope
corpus posuit.

erat in manu.

erat in ore.

erat prope

pedes.

Activity Suggestions

While this guide and the online resources do include a variety of activities, there are more activities teachers can use to supplement and give students understandable messages in Latin. We give many thanks to the teachers who share their materials and suggestions for activities. All of these resources are provided with permission.

Activity	URL	Brief Abstract
Movie Short	http://goo.gl/Z48ewk	Using a movie short or movie clip, teach students new vocabulary and reinforce learned vocabulary.
Running Dictation	http://goo.gl/FrGCke	Instead of delivering a dictation to students, have them deliver it to each other!
Parallel Universe	http://goo.gl/5znGuC	Use details to review a story and write your own version.
4 Word Picture	http://goo.gl/0YIJ3m	Give students 4 words and let them draw pictures to use for circling and story-telling.
Draw 1-2-3	https://goo.gl/F9AvnX	A reading, writing, drawing, and critical thinking activity that works much like a movie short, but with pictures
One Word at a Time Stories	https://goo.gl/XUofZH	Using one word at a time, students write compelling stories to share.

Capitulum I - Pluto

Activity	Location	QR Code (if applicable)
Word Cloud	Teacher's Guide Book	
Chapter 1 Dictatio	https://goo.gl/aEfgxV	
Chapter 1 Audio	https://goo.gl/8XbcpC	
Publius Publicanus Cards[4]	Cards: Teacher's Guide Book Instructions: https://goo.gl/u2q6gu	
Chapter One Reading Guide	Teacher's Guide Book	

[4] Credit to this activity is given to Alina Filipescu. Original post can be found here: http://tprsforchinese.blogspot.com/2015/09/pancho-camacho-game.html

Chapter 1 - Word Cloud

Publius Publicanus Cards

puer

mortuus

nemo

puella

deus

rex

tristis

sapiens

stultus

pulcher

soror

frater

amícus

coníunx

Capitulum Primum

Vocabula Nova

Keep track of new words you learn here.

Picturae

Pinge tres picturas de capitulo
Label everything; no captions allowed

Quaestiones

Responde Latine quaestionibus de capitulo

1. describe Plutonem.

2. quis Plutonem amat?

3. quid Iuppiter habet quod Pluto non habet?

4. quem Pluto amat? describe eam.

Capitulum II - Proserpina

Activity	Location	QR Code (if applicable)
Word Cloud	Teacher's Guide Book	
Chapter 2 Total Physical Response Review	Teacher's Guide Book	
Chapter 2 Audio	https://goo.gl/J2Tbkx	
Chapter 2 Fly Killer Game	https://goo.gl/OCg2KH	
Chapter 2 Reading Guide	Teacher's Guide Book	

Chapter 2 - Word Cloud

Capitulum II TPR Review

Verbs	Nouns	Descriptors
ambulare	ianua	ferociter
currere	mensula	tristis
considere	charta	crudelis
surgere	amicus amica	laetus
ponere deponere reponere	discipulus discipula	iratus
vertere	liber	mortuus
tangere	tabula	perterritus
pulsare	puer puella	sapiens
capere	stylus peniculus	stultus

Nomen: _____   Sessio: ____   Datum: _____

Capitulum Secundum

Vocabula Nova

Keep track of new words you learn here.

Picturae

Pinge tres picturas de capitulo
Label everything; no captions allowed

Quaestiones

Responde Latine quaestionibus de capitulo

1. describe Proserpinam.

2. quid mater Proserpinae vocatur?

3. quem mater amavit ante Proserpinam? quem mater amat iam?

4. quid Proserpinae agere placet?

Capitulum III - Pluto

Activity	Location	QR Code (if applicable)
Word Cloud	Teacher's Guide Book	
Chapter 3 Dictatio/Pictatio	https://goo.gl/OuGYlq	
Chapter 3 Audio	https://goo.gl/1sXi05	
Chapter 3 Dramatic Tableaux[5]	handouts: Teacher's Guide Book instructions: https://goo.gl/bqbSCx	
Chapter 3 Reading Guide	Teacher's Guide Book	

---

[5] credit for this activity given to Drama Resource. Original instructions can be found here: http://dramaresource.com/tableaux/

Chapter 3 - Word Cloud

Chapter 3 - Dramatic Tableaux

nomina: _____ Sessio:_____ Datum:_____

*Explicatio: You will create a still shot of your scene. Imagine if you press pause on a video you are watching. As a group, consider these questions below and stage your scene. When it is your turn, you will present your scene. **Nota Bene**: each person should have something to say when he or she is tapped! This will allow us to figure out your scene.*

Build	
Write 3-5 sentences in English about your scene. Who is in it? What is happening?	
Determine who will be what in your scene. If you are showing action, more than one person may be a character. *e.g. if Jupiter is attacking his father, you might have a before and after freeze frame.*	
Each person should have one sentence that they will say out loud when they are tapped. This sentence should let us, the audience, know who is who and what is happening. Write out your sentences here.	
Reflect	
Why is your scene important?	
Choose one character or interaction from your scene. What does this tell us about our story?	

Scenes

sum deus. sum rex. sum rex mortuorum. sub terra habito. habito cum mortuis. fratrem habeo; Iuppiter vocatur. sororem habeo; Iuno vocatur. dei in caelo habitant. nemo me amat. die me puerum deridebant. Iuppiter est rex mortalium et me deridebat. Iuno est dea pulchra et me deridebat. iam dei sun amici, sed nemo me amat.

Iuppiter coniugem habebat… minime… Iuppiter multas amicas et coniugem habebat. coniugem habere volo. coniugem pulchram et sapientem volo. nolo coniugem stultam habere. frater me non intellegit et mihi dicit, "cur tristis es? familiam et amicos habes!" frater meus est stultus.

unam amo. puella est pulchra et sapiens. puella est pulchrior quam omnes dei. puella est sapientior quam omnes dei. olim eam video in terra. video puellam in terra ambulare et flores sumere. donum puellae dare volo, sed timeo.

sum puella et dea. mater mea Ceres vocatur. mater est dea terrae. mater me ferociter amat. matrem ferociter amo. terram amo. terram et matrem et flores et amicas et animalia amo. amo in terra ambulare et flores sumere. amo matrem mihi fabulas dicere.

pater meus Iuppiter vocatur. in caelo habitat, sed in terra laborat. pater meus mortales amat. mortales non amo. mortales terram necant. ego terram amo! terram et matrem et flores et amicas et animalia amo. mortales non amo!

mater me rogavit, "visne te coniugem esse?" matrem non intellegebam. mater mihi inquit, "tu es puella. es puella pulchra et dea. dei te volunt facere coniugem esse. visne coniugem esse?" matrem intellexi et dixi coniugem esse nolle. mater inquit, "optime".

mater mihi fabulam dicit. mater Iovem amabat sed Iuppiter matrem meam non amavit. non intellego cur Iuppiter esset crudelis. Iuppiter coniugem habebat, sed coniunx non erat mater. iam, mater neminem amat sed me solam.

fratrem in terra video. frater currit. nolo currere sed volo fratri dicere. currere fratri placet. mihi non placet. libros legere mihi placet. frater erat athleticus, ego non. multae puellae fratrem amo, me non. frater coniugem habet, ego non.

volo fratri dicere et fratrem agito. frater in terra currit. inquam (I say), "frater, coniugem habere volo." frater inquit, "coniugem. quis erit?" fabulam dico. puella est pulchra et sapiens. puella est pulchrior quam omnes dei et sapientior quam omnes dei. volo eam coniugem facere. frater ridet et inquit, "certe frater. iam, librum lege. volo currere."

Capitulum Tertium

Vocabula Nova
Keep track of new words you learn here.

Dictatio/Pictatio

sententia prima I	pictura	sententia secunda II	pictura
sententia tertia III	pictura	sententia quarta IV	pictura
sententia quinta V	pictura	sententia sexta VI	pictura

Quaestiones

Responde Latine quaestionibus de capitulo

1. ubi erat Iuppiter?

2. quid Iuppiter agebat?

3. quid Plutoni agere placebat?

4. quid Pluto Iovi dixit?

5. quo modo Iuppiter Plutoni respondit?

Capitulum IV - Proserpina

Activity	Location	QR Code (if applicable)
Word Cloud	Teacher's Guide Book	
Chapter 4 Audio	https://goo.gl/L3ihOc	
Timeline	Passages: Teacher's Guide Instructions: https://goo.gl/w6V7jJ	
Sentence Frames	Teacher's Guide Book	
Chapter 4 Reading Guide	Teacher's Guide Book	

Chapter 4 - World Cloud

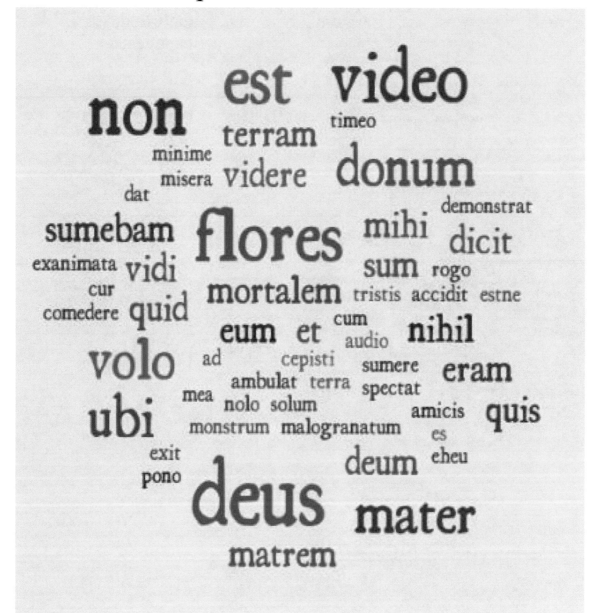

Chapter 4 - Timeline Passages

★ puerum, dei Plutonem deridebant. Pluto sororem et fratrem habebat. soror Iuno vocabatur et erat pulchra. frater Iuppiter vocabatur et erat rex mortalium. soror et frater Plutonem deridebant.

★ Pluto sub terra habitabat. dei in caelo habitabant. mortales in terra habitabant. mortui sub terra habitabant. nemo Plutonem amabat: nec dei nec mortales nec mortui. Pluto coniugem volebat.

★ Pluto unam amabat. erat puella pulchra et sapiens. puella erat pulchrior et sapientior quam omnes dei. Pluto puellam in terra vidit. puella flores sumebat.

★ Proserpina erat puella pulchra. mater Ceres vocabatur et erat dea terrae. Proserpina terram et matrem et flores et amicas et animalia amabat.

★ Iuppiter in terra currebat. Pluto, frater, Iovem agitabat quod Pluto fratri dicere volebat. Iovi currere placebat. Plutoni currere non placebat. Plutoni legere placebat.

★ Pluto Iovi dixit coniugem habere velle. Iuppiter ridebat et inquit, "certe. iam lege! volo currere."

★ Proserpina in terra flores sumebat. Proserpina erat cum amicis. Proserpina terram et amicas et flores vidit. subito, Proserpina mortalem vidit, sed non erat mortalem, erat deus Pluto.

★ Proserpina non erat in terra. Proserpina matrem et flores et terram non vidit. Proserpina timebat. Proserpina *meminit (remembered)* in terra esse et flores sumere.

★ Proserpina deum audiebat. deus ad Proserpinam ambulabat. Proserpina timebat. Proserpina rogavit, "quis es? cur me cepisti? ubi est mater?" sed deus nihil dixit.

★ Pluto nihil dixit et ad Proserpinam ambulabat. Pluto donum habebat. donum erat malogranatum. Pluto donum demonstrabat Proserpinae.

★ Proserpina donum *accepit (accepted)*. donum erat malogranatum. Proserpina donum in solo posuit. Proserpina malogranatum comedere nolebat.

Chapter 4 - Sentence Frames

1. olim per _____
    (place) ambulabam.

2. subito, _____
    (person/monster) me agitabat et me
    cepit!

3. exanimatus/a eram et in
    _____ (other place)
    excitavi.

4. tandem fugi quod sum
    _____ (adjective) quam
    _____ (person/monster).

42

Capitulum Quartum

Vocabula Nova
Keep track of new words you learn here.

Picturae
On the back, put these events in order and draw a simple picture to represent each.

Pluto Proserpinam cepit.	Proserpina Plutonem sub terra audivit.	Proserpina sub terra excitavit.	Pluto Proserpinae donum demonstravit.
Proserpina flores sumebat.	Proserpina Plutonem sub terra vidit.	Pluto donum in terram posuit et exiit.	Pluto Proserpinae nihil dixit.

Sententiae Falsae
What is false about each statement?

1. Proserpina matrem et flores sub terra vidit.
2. Pluto flores in terra sumebat.
3. Pluto erat mortalis.
4. Proserpina donum Plutoni habebat.
5. Proserpina malogranatum comedere volebat.

Capitulum V - Proserpina

Activity	Location	QR Code (if applicable)
Word Cloud	Teacher's Guide Book	
Chapter 5 Audio	https://goo.gl/Ia63kY	
Seek and Find	Handout: Teacher's Guide Instructions: http://goo.gl/GhzdVe	
Chapter 5 Reading Guide	Teacher's Guide Book	

Chapter 5 - Word Cloud

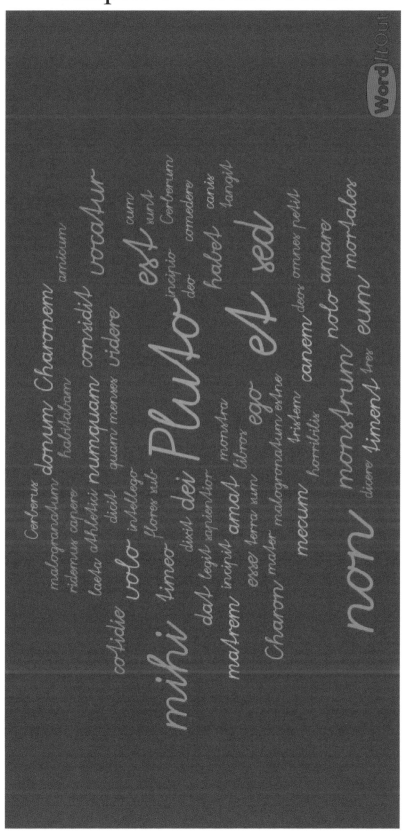

Chapter 5 - Seek and Find

Pluto canem habet. Cerberus vocatur.	eum non intellego. / sed monstrum non est.	Pluto vocatur.
Pluto mecum considit cotidie.	mortales Charonem et Cerberum timent.	inicipit mihi dicere.
numquam me petit.	mecum considit et mihi dicit.	numquam me tangit.
nolo donum capere.	sed nolo eum tristem esse.	eum amare incipio.
mater mihi dixit.	deos monstra esse et me non amare	mihi libros legit.
matrem videre volo.	Pluto mihi flores dat.	Pluto me amat.
Pluto amicum habet. Charon vocatur.	Pluto est sapientior quam omnes dei.	laeta sum.

Capitulum Quintum

Vocabula Nova
Keep track of new words you learn here.

Picturae
Draw a picture of each character below as they are described in capitulo quinto.

Cerberus et Charon	Proserpina	Pluto

Quaestiones
Consider these questions. Use the text to build your answers.

1. Describe Pluto's world. How is it changing?

2. In Chapter 1, Pluto feels utterly lonely, how is that changing? How is Proserpina causing that change?

3. What is Proserpina's struggle? What changes are happening within her to cause this?

Capitulum VI - Pluto

Activity	Location	QR Code (if applicable)
Word Cloud	Teacher's Guide Book	
Chapter 6 Audio	https://goo.gl/c9WYS0	
Chapter 6 Dictatio	https://goo.gl/YRQqDp	
Chapter 6 Serpens Activity[6]	Teacher's Guide Book https://goo.gl/ezHxYP	
Chapter 6 Reading Guide	Teacher's Guide Book	

---

[6] This activity makes use of Standards. The blank boxes are for teachers to fill in standards or guidelines for students. The activity is provided here in print as well as with an url.

Chapter 6 - Word Cloud

Serpens

Choose one activity from each row. Each activity needs to touch the last either diagonally or vertically. **Make sure you ONLY USE Chapters 1-6!!!!!**

Standards/Skills	Activity Options		
	Draw your favorite moment from the story. Use **Latin** captions to make the drawing clear.	Translate three lines of the story into very good English.	Rewrite six lines of the story in a modern day setting in English.
	Choose five **Latin** words from the story, and give an English derivative (word that comes from Latin) for each, with its definition.	Choose five **Latin** words from the story, and give an English derivative for each, and illustrate the derivatives.	Choose five **Latin** words from the story, and give an English derivative for each, and write a sentence in English using each derivative.
	Write two sentences in **Latin**, and each one describes a character in the story.	Write a summary of your favourite chapter in **Latin**. Keep it short; 3 sentences.	Write and illustrate a comic in **Latin** that summarizes your favourite chapter. Only 3 sentences.
	Write four questions in **Latin** about one of the chapters we've read in the story and find another student to answer them.	Answer four questions in **Latin** that another student wrote about one of the chapters we've read in the story.	Write three questions in **Latin** with their answers in **Latin** about one of the chapters we've read in the story.
	Using the sentences in the story to help you, write at least three sentences in **Latin** that predict what you think will happen next.	Using the sentences in the story to help you, construct five sentences about the scene in **Latin** two of which are true and one of which is false.	Using the sentences in the story to help you, create a poem in **Latin** about any of the characters in the play.

Capitulum Sextum

Vocabula Nova
Keep track of new words you learn here.

Picturae
Pinge tres picturas de capitulo
Label everything; no captions allowed

Quaestiones
Responde Latine quaestionibus de capitulo

1. describe Tartarum ante Proserpinam.

2. describe Tartarum *cum* (when) Proserpina *ibi (there)* sit.

3. quis advenit?

4. quid est difficultas?

Capitulum Septimum - Proserpina

Activity	Location	QR Code (if applicable)
Word Cloud	Teacher's Guide Book	
Chapter 7 Audio	https://goo.gl/7r1wZD	
Chapter 7 Lactuca Game	https://goo.gl/jBkZN4	
Chapter 6 Reading Guide	Teacher's Guide Book	

Chapter 7 - Word Cloud

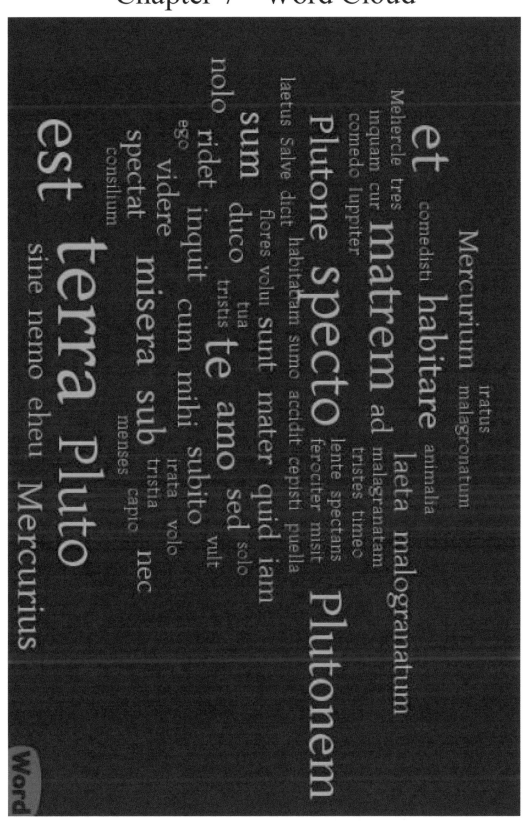

Capitulum Septimum

Vocabula Nova

Keep track of new words you learn here.

Picturae

Pinge tres picturas de capitulo
Label everything; no captions allowed

Sententiae Falsae

Circle what is false about each statement.

1. Iuppiter Proserpinam videre volebat.
2. Ceres erat misera et laeta.
3. Proserpina sine Plutone habitare volebat.
4. Pluto malogranatum cepit et comedit.
5. Pluto Proserpinam non amabat.

Capitulum Octavum - Proserpina

Activity	Location	QR Code (if applicable)
Word Cloud	Teacher's Guide Book	
Chapter 8 Audio	https://goo.gl/7r1wZD	
Chapter 8 Character Cards	Teacher's Guide Book	
Chapter 8 Reading Guide	Teacher's Guide Book	

Chapter 8 - Word Cloud

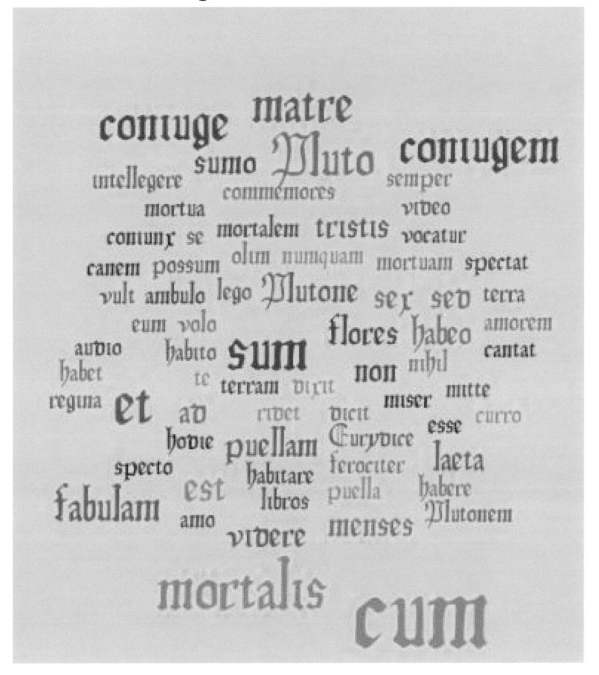

Capitulum Octavum-Character Cards

Create two (2) character cards for the characters Pluto and Proserpina. Each card should represent the character in a different stage of the book (Pluto - chapters 1 and 8; Proserpina - chapters 2 and 8). Write 7-10 sentences for each card in Latin about the character and then draw a picture that accurately depicts the character at that time.

Pluto in capitulo primo	*sententiae:*	*pictura:*
Pluto in capitulo octavo	*sententiae:*	*pictura:*
Proserpina in capitulo secundo	*sententiae:*	*pictura:*
Proserpina in capitulo octavo	*sententiae:*	*pictura:*

Capitulum Octavum

Vocabula Nova

Keep track of new words you learn here.

Picturae

Draw a picture of the characters as you think of them now at the end of the book. Write one line from the book that you think sums up the character.

Pluto	Proserpina	Ceres

Quaestiones Totae Fabulae

Consider these questions now that you've read the entire book.

1. Is Pluto an anti-hero, a villain, or a hero? How do you know?

2. What does this story tell us about Roman perspectives and mythology?

3. What do you know about the story of Eurydice? What do you think happens when Pluto releases her to her husband?

57045228R00039

Made in the USA
Charleston, SC
05 June 2016